Comptroller of the Currency
Administrator of National Banks

Country Risk Management

Comptroller's Handbook

March 2008

Other Areas of Examination Interest

Country Risk Management

Table of Contents

Introduction

Overview

Financial institutions increasingly do business abroad to diversify and expand their sources of revenue and profitability. This strategy exposes the bank to country risk and raises the potential for financial loss. Country risk is the risk that economic, social, and political conditions and events in a foreign country will affect an institution. To manage this risk, banks must institute adequate systems and controls over their international activities.

Banks' international activities vary considerably. Some of the largest banks provide a wide range of financial products and services through foreign branches, wholly owned banks, joint venture banks, representative offices, and affiliates. Their clients are often local affiliates or branches of the largest global conglomerates, as well as large local firms, and, increasingly, consumers (retail banking). In contrast, regional banks and branches of foreign banks[1] are exposed to international activities primarily by serving the needs of their domestic, corporate clients. Some small banks engage in trade finance and correspondent banking and may have close ties to certain geographic areas, such as Latin America, Asia, or the Middle East.

Given the wide-range in banks' international activities and foreign countries' different policies and conditions, this booklet provides examiners with the basic elements of the country risk management process. This booklet also describes procedures to evaluate the adequacy of banks' systems and controls for managing risks from international activities. Examiners must use judgment in applying these procedures and should calibrate their examinations to bank size, as well as volume and complexity of international activities.

---

[1] This booklet focuses on banks rather than branches of foreign banks; however, the concepts articulated herein are also relevant to these branches. For more information, please see the December 1999 *Comptroller's Handbook*, "Federal Branches and Agencies Supervision."

Risks Associated with International Activities

Under the OCC's supervision-by-risk philosophy, risk is the potential that expected and unexpected events may adversely impact banks' earnings or capital, and banks engaged in international activities are exposed to country risk. For example, in the past, foreign obligors have experienced financial difficulties due to adverse economic conditions and defaulted because of nationalization or expropriation of assets, directed lending, government repudiation of external indebtedness (sovereign risk), exchange controls,[2] and currency depreciation or devaluation. Country risk concerns have, on occasion, spread to other countries as markets became concerned about countries that exhibited similar characteristics.

Although country risk is separate from the OCC's nine categories of risk for bank supervision,[3] financial institutions should consider all categories of risk when implementing a country risk management process. Country risk takes a comprehensive view of the risks inherent in international activities, including how banks are affected by country-specific or regional factors. This applies to loans and other credit exposures but also to international capital market transactions (e.g., foreign exchange, derivatives, and swaps), investments in foreign subsidiaries, electronic banking agreements, and information technology servicing and other outsourcing arrangements with foreign providers.

Country risk applies to cross-border operations as well as local currency/in-country operations. In the past, risk from cross-border operations (the inability to transfer or convert local currencies into other currencies) was the most prominent international risk impacting debt repayment. In recent years, risks associated with local currency exposure have increased in prominence. For example, while traditionally a U.S. bank likely had only a minimal share of a foreign market, now it might have a significant market share. Banks with

---

[2] Exchange controls fall under transfer risk, which is a facet of country risk. Transfer risk is the possibility that an asset cannot be serviced in the currency of payment because the obligor's country lacks the necessary foreign exchange or has put restraints on its availability. The Interagency Country Exposure Review Committee assigns ratings to foreign exposures based on its evaluation of the level of transfer risk associated with a country. See the *Guide to the Interagency Country Exposure Review Committee Process*, issued in November 1999, for a comprehensive discussion of the operations of the Interagency Country Exposure Review Committee.

[3] Definitions for OCC's nine categories of risk can be found in Appendix H, "Categories of Risk" in the September 2007 *Comptroller's Handbook*, "Bank Supervision Process."

operations in foreign countries face reputation and regulatory/compliance risks from local supervisors and press coverage, both of which tend to increase as the size of banks' in-country operations and market shares expand. Banks also face local liquidity, credit, interest rate, price and operational risks, all of which should be addressed within a comprehensive country risk management framework.

Country risk is not limited to a financial institution's exposure to foreign-domiciled counterparties. Country risk factors should also be considered, where feasible, when assessing domestic counterparties. For instance, country risk would affect exposures to U.S.-domiciled counterparties if the creditworthiness of the borrower or of a guarantor (or the value of the collateral) is significantly impacted by events in a foreign country.

Elements of an Effective Country Risk Management Process

To effectively control the level of risk associated with international activities, banks must have a risk management process that focuses on the broadly defined concept of country risk. A sound country risk management process includes

- Oversight by the board of directors,
- Written risk management policies and procedures,
- A system for reporting country exposures,
- A process for analyzing country risk,
- A country risk rating system,
- Country exposure limits,
- Monitoring of country conditions,
- Stress testing and integrated scenario planning, and
- Internal controls and audit function.

Although country risk management processes vary from one bank to the next, the processes must be commensurate with the volume and complexity of banks' international activities. Supervisory expectations will also vary based on the scope of international activities.

Oversight by the Board of Directors

The board of directors must ensure that country risk is managed effectively.[4] The board is responsible for periodically reviewing and approving policies governing the bank's international activities to ensure that they are appropriate and consistent with the bank's strategic plans, goals, risk tolerance, and strength of capital and management. Bank policy should clarify and quantify strategic goals and risk parameters, including country risk. Where the bank uses economic[5] or regulatory capital to control and manage country exposure, the board should evaluate and approve the allocations. Also, through appropriate reporting processes, the board should evaluate how effectively bank management controls country risk.

Policies and Procedures for Managing Country Risk

Bank management is responsible for developing and implementing sound, well-defined policies and procedures for managing country risk. The policies and procedures should address the following:

- Articulate a strategy for doing business abroad, and identify the major risks in a particular country and region. The strategy should cover product and service offerings and types of legal vehicles (e.g., branches, banks, affiliates, joint ventures) to be pursued.

- Delineate clear lines of responsibility and accountability for country risk management decisions with an appropriate balance between in-country managers, regional management committees, and headquarters risk management.

- Establish risk tolerance limits, reporting and measurement processes, and exception procedures.

---

[4] Depending on bank size and complexity, the board of directors may delegate board functions to board committees. See Chapter II of the OCC's "Directors' Book" in the *National Bank Directors' Toolkit*.

[5] Economic capital refers to a bank's internal assessment of the capital needed to support the risk in its activities, that is, the amount of capital necessary to minimize the likelihood of the bank failing. Economic capital is distinct from familiar accounting and regulatory capital measures and is a potentially more forward-looking measure of capital adequacy.

- Require periodic reporting of country risk exposures and limit exceptions to senior management and the board of directors.

Management should also ensure that country risk management policies and procedures are clearly communicated and fully implemented.

Country Exposure Reporting System

To effectively manage country risk, the bank must have a reliable reporting system for capturing and categorizing the volume and nature of foreign exposures. The system should cover all aspects of the bank's operations, including cross-border and in-country exposures. In addition to its critical role in risk management, an accurate and timely reporting system is necessary to support the regulatory reporting of foreign exposures on the Federal Financial Institutions Examination Council's quarterly Country Exposure Report.[6]

The board of directors should regularly receive reports on the level of foreign exposures. If the level of foreign exposures in the bank is significant, or if a country to which the bank is exposed is considered to be high risk, exposures should be reported to the board at least quarterly. More frequent reporting is appropriate when there are concentrations[7] or deterioration in foreign exposures would threaten the earnings, capital, and/or reputation of the bank.

Country Risk Analysis Process

Although the nature of the country risk analysis process and level of resources devoted to the process vary depending on the size and sophistication of the bank's international operations, several questions should be considered when evaluating the process in all banks:

- Is there a quantitative and qualitative assessment of the risk associated with each country in which the bank is conducting or planning to conduct business?

---

[6] Form FFIEC 009.

[7] For purposes of this handbook, concentrations that exceed 25 percent of the bank's Tier 1 capital plus the allowance for loan and lease losses are considered to be significant; however, in some cases, lesser degrees of exposure may also be considered significant.

- Is a formal analysis of country risk conducted at least annually, and does the bank have an effective system for monitoring interim developments?

- Does the analysis take into account all material aspects of the broadly defined concept of country risk, as well as any special risks associated with specific groups of counterparties the bank may have targeted in its business strategy?

- Does the bank consider short- and long-term early warning analyses performed by third parties and information provided by in-country managers?

- Is the analysis adequately documented, and are conclusions concerning the level of risk communicated in a way that provides decision makers with a reasonable basis for determining the nature and level of the bank's exposures in a country?

- Given the size and sophistication of the bank's international activities, are the resources devoted to the country risk management and analysis process, including quantitative models, adequate?

- As a final check of the process, are the bank's conclusions concerning a country reasonable in light of information available from other sources, including external research and rating agencies?

Conclusions about the level of country risk should reflect an evaluation of the effect of prevailing and potential economic, political, and social conditions on counterparties. The appendix to this handbook describes these factors in more detail.

Country Risk Ratings

Trends in country risk ratings and underlying analyses should be understood and related to the level of exposure and capital at risk. This will help in assessing the risk-reward relationship and enable a better understanding of management's risk tolerance.

Because some counterparties may be more exposed to local country conditions than others, it is a common and acceptable practice for banks to distinguish among different types of exposures when assigning country risk ratings. For example, trade-related and banking sector exposures may receive better risk ratings than other categories of exposure. This is because the importance of these types of transactions to a country's economy has usually moved governments to give them preferential treatment for repayment.

The risk rating systems of some banks may differentiate between public versus private sector exposures. And in some banks, a country's private sector credits cannot be rated less severely than its public sector credits (i.e., the bank imposes a "sovereign ceiling" on the rating for all exposures in a country). Both are acceptable practices.

The Interagency Country Exposure Review Committee's ratings focus only on transfer risk (see footnote 2) and are used by supervisors to assign reserves against transfer risk. In contrast, bank-determined country risk ratings reflect a broader set of risks (e.g., currency depreciation/devaluation, expropriation, default, directed lending) and guide banks in managing existing exposures. Such ratings should, therefore, have a forward-looking and broad country risk focus.

Country Exposure Limits

As part of their country risk management process, internationally active banks should adopt a system of country exposure limits.[8] Limits may be expressed in dollars or as a percentage of capital. Because the limit-setting process often involves divergent interests within the bank (such as those of business managers, the bank's overall country risk manager, and the country risk committee), country risk limits usually reflect several considerations, including

- The overall business strategy that guides international activities,
- The country's risk rating and the bank's appetite for risk,
- Perceived business opportunities in the country, and
- The desire to support the international business needs of domestic customers.

---

[8] Some banks use guidelines, which tend to be less formal than limits. Proper escalation policies and approval of excesses are essential in either case.

Limits should be approved by the board of directors and communicated to all affected departments and staff. They should be reviewed and approved at least annually and more frequently when concerns about a particular country arise.

Internationally active banks should consider supplementing their aggregate exposure limits with more discrete controls. Such controls might take the form of limits on the different lines of business in the various countries, limits by type of counterparties, or limits by type or tenor of exposure. Banks might also limit exposure to local currencies. Banks that have both substantial capital market exposures and credit-related exposures typically set separate aggregate exposure limits for each because exposures to the two lines of business are usually measured differently.

Although country-by-country exposure limits are customary, banks should assess correlations due to common systemic factors and place limits on a broader portfolio basis. A troubled country's problems often affect its neighbors, and adverse effects may extend to geographically distant countries with close economic ties, similar debt profiles, or similar economic, capital market and financial system structures. By monitoring and controlling exposures on a regional or portfolio basis, banks are in a better position to respond if the adverse effects of a country's problems begin to spread.

For banks engaged primarily in direct lending activities, compliance with country exposure limits should be monitored regularly and routinely. However, banks with more volatile portfolios, including those with significant trading accounts, should increase monitoring. Exceptions to country exposure limits should be reported to an appropriate level of management or to the board so they can be approved or corrective measures considered.

Monitoring Country Conditions

Banks should have a system for monitoring current credit and capital market conditions. The level of resources devoted to monitoring country conditions should be proportionate to the level of exposure and the perceived level of risk. Further, banks should monitor regional conditions/trends or monitor a group of countries with similar characteristics.

If banks maintain in-country offices, reports from local staff are a resource for monitoring country conditions. Periodic country visits by regional or country managers are important for monitoring individual exposures and country conditions. Banks may draw on information from rating agencies and other external sources.

Senior management and the responsible country managers should be in communication regularly. Banks should not rely solely on informal lines of communication and *ad hoc* decision making in times of crisis. As country conditions deteriorate, institutions should increase the frequency of monitoring.

Stress Testing and Integrated Scenario Planning

Procedures should be in place for stress testing and integrated scenario planning.[9] This involves early identification of potential country risk problems and handling of exposures in troubled countries, including contingency plans for mitigating or reducing risk and, if necessary, exiting the country.

Banks should periodically stress-test their foreign exposures and report the results to their boards of directors and senior management. Stress testing does not necessarily refer to the use of sophisticated financial modeling tools but rather to the need for all banks to evaluate the potential impact of different scenarios on their country risk profiles.

Banks with high levels of international exposure should consider applying scenarios and stress tests across countries, business lines, and products using assumptions that are applicable to the type of business conducted, country, and region.

An integrated scenario planning process should incorporate contingency plans. The level of resources devoted to this effort should be commensurate with the significance of foreign exposures in the bank's overall operations.

---

[9] See *International Convergence of Capital Measurement and Capital Standards: A Revised Framework, Comprehensive Version,* "Stress Tests Used in Assessment of Capital Adequacy" (June 2006, page 96 and the following pages). See also "Stress Testing at Major Financial Institutions: Survey Results and Practice," Bank for International Settlements (CGFS Publications, No. 24, January 2005).

Internal Controls and Audit

The bank's board of directors and senior management should ensure that the country risk management process includes effective internal control processes. In addition, the bank's audit program should provide an opinion as to the integrity and accuracy of the information used by the board and senior management to monitor compliance with country risk policies and exposure limits. The system of internal controls should detect noncompliance with policy and limits. They should ensure, for example, that the responsibilities of marketing and lending personnel are properly segregated from the responsibilities of personnel who analyze country risk, rate country risk, and set country limits. The control system should also include a unit self-assessment process.

For additional guidance and requirements regarding management and board responsibilities for establishing and maintaining an effective internal control structure, refer to the "Internal and External Audits" booklet of the *Comptroller's Handbook*.

Examination Procedures

General Procedures

These procedures are intended to determine the adequacy of the bank's policies, procedures, and internal controls as they relate to country risk management. The extent of testing and procedures performed should be based upon the examiner's assessment of risk. This assessment should include consideration of work performed by other regulatory agencies, internal and external auditors, internal compliance review units, formalized policies and procedures, and the effectiveness of internal controls and management information systems.

Objective: Determine the scope of the examination of the bank's country risk management process and identify examination activities necessary to meet the needs of the supervisory strategy for the bank.

1. Review the following documents for any previously identified problems that require follow-up:

   ❑ Supervisory strategy.
   ❑ EIC's scope memorandum.
   ❑ Previous Report of Examination.
   ❑ Working papers from the previous examination.
   ❑ Internal and external audit reports, management responses and follow-up reports and, if necessary, work papers.
   ❑ Correspondence.

2. Review the bank's recent FFIEC 009 Country Exposure Reports and relevant qualitative and quantitative internal bank reports for any apparent changes, trends, or areas of concern in the bank's international activities.

3. Obtain from International Banking and Finance any information that may be relevant to the bank's international activities.

4. Obtain and review the following documents to determine the amount of oversight provided for the bank's international activities:

❑ A list of board and senior management committees that supervise the bank's international activities, including a list of members and meeting schedules. Also review copies of the minutes documenting the meetings of these groups since the last examination.

❑ Reports related to the bank's international activities and country exposures that have been furnished to the board of directors, country risk management committee, or any similar committee.

5. Obtain and review policy and procedure manuals, reports, and any other tools used by management to supervise the bank's international activities, including

❑ Organization chart.
❑ Written policy and procedure manuals.
❑ Strategic and business plans for international activities.
❑ List of products, services, and business initiatives.
❑ Due diligence or risk assessments for new products or services.
❑ Country limit and exposure reports, including exposure of sovereigns to legal lending limits (12 CFR 32.5(f)).
❑ Country risk analysis and rating reports.
❑ Concentration reports.
❑ Exception reports.
❑ Reports on the results of any financial modeling tools and stress tests/scenario analyses that may have been applied to the bank's international portfolio.

6. Through discussions with management and review of request information, identify any areas of significant change or possible concern in the bank's international activities, including

- Any significant changes in policies, procedures, or personnel.
- Any significant changes in the products offered, size of exposures, or market focus.
- The level and trend in delinquencies and losses.
- Any significant changes in the level of concentrations or the number of exceptions granted to established limits.

- Any internal or external factors that could affect the level of risk associated with the bank's international activities, including:
  — Changes in country exposure limits.
  — Economic conditions in the countries and regions in which the bank has exposure.

7. Using the information obtained while performing these procedures and from discussions with the bank EIC, determine the scope of this examination and its objectives.

Select steps necessary to meet objectives from the following examination procedures. Seldom will every step be required.

Quantity of Risk

Conclusion: The quantity of risk is (low, moderate, high).

Objective: To determine the level of country risk associated with the bank's international activities.

1. Analyze the volume and distribution of the bank's international activities, including commitments and other off-balance-sheet exposures, noting any changes since the previous examination. Determine the implications for risk of the following:

   - Significant country or regional concentrations of exposure.
   - Serious economic or other problems in countries in which the bank has significant exposures.
   - Significant growth in exposures to residents of a particular country.
   - Significant growth in exposures to a particular economic sector within a country (e.g., banking, commodity producers, manufacturing, or the public sector).
   - Significant growth in exposures to a geographic region (e.g., Asia, Latin America, or Eastern Europe).
   - Significant growth in any existing products or activities.
   - Any new or planned products or activities.

2. Analyze the type, mix, and sources of local, in-country funding sources, noting any changes since the previous examination. Consider reliance on short-term, high-cost, or borrowed funds, sources of contingency funds, and expectations for, and management of, large inflows or outflows of funds.

3. Evaluate exposures to sovereigns and determine compliance with the legal lending limit (12 CFR 32.5(f)).

4. If the bank has acquired any significant new foreign affiliates since the previous examination, analyze the effect of these acquisitions on the risk profile of the bank. Consider

   - The nature and volume of the affiliate's activities.

- The affiliate's potential for adversely affecting the bank's reputation.

5. Review the business and/or strategic plan for the bank's international activities. Consider

    - Growth goals and exposure limits for individual countries and for regions.
    - New and planned products and business lines.

6. Review and discuss with management any internally prepared risk assessments of the bank's international activities.

Quality of Risk Management

Conclusion: The quality of risk management is (strong, satisfactory, weak).

Policy

Conclusion: The board (has/has not) established effective policies to manage the level of country risk associated with the bank's international activities.

Objective: To determine whether the bank has established and effectively communicated the policies, standards, and procedures necessary to manage the country risk associated with its international activities.

1. Evaluate relevant policies to determine whether they provide appropriate guidance for the bank's international activities. Consider

   - Country risk tolerance (i.e., the maximum acceptable country risk rating).
   - Authorized lines of business.
   - Approved instruments and terms.
   - Desirable and undesirable types of business.

2. Review the process used to establish country exposure limits. Consider

   - The role of the country risk management committee, the chief country risk management officer, country managers, and marketing staff in setting country exposure limits.
   - The process for reviewing and approving country exposure limits.
   - The process for approving exceptions to country exposure limits.

3. Determine whether country exposure limits are well-defined and reasonable. Consider

   - The way limits are measured. (For example, is capital or some other standard used to define the exposure limit?)

- The relationship between assigned ratings and the bank's system for establishing country exposure limits.
- The use of sub-limits for different types and terms of exposure within a country.
- The use of regional or portfolio limits as a tool for limiting the effects of a contagion of problems between countries.
- The impact on the bank if the country exposure limit is reached.

4. Evaluate the policy review and country exposure limit approval processes to ensure that the policy and/or exposure limits can be adjusted in response to changes in the level of country risk.

5. Determine whether the board of directors has approved the current policies and country exposure limits.

6. While performing the remaining procedures, evaluate whether country risk management policies and exposure limits have been clearly communicated to affected staff.

Processes

Conclusion: The bank (does/does not) have systems in place to provide accurate and timely assessments of the country risk associated with its international activities.

Objective: To determine whether the bank has systems in place to provide accurate and timely assessments of the country risk associated with its international activities.

1. Review the bank's definition of country risk and determine whether it broadly covers the concept of country risk.

2. In light of the size and sophistication of the bank's international activities, evaluate the adequacy of the bank's country risk analysis process. Consider

- Does the bank assess the level of risk associated with each country in which it is currently conducting or planning to do business?

- Is a formal analysis of country risk conducted at least annually, and does the bank have an effective system for monitoring developments in the interim?
- Does the bank's analysis take into account all aspects of the broadly defined concept of country risk, as well as any special risks associated with specific groups of counterparties the bank may have targeted in its business strategy?
- Is the bank's analysis adequately documented, and are its conclusions concerning the level of risk communicated in a way that provides decision makers with a reasonable basis for determining the nature and level of the bank's exposures in a country?
- Are the resources devoted to the country risk analysis process, including the number and expertise of staff, considered adequate?
- Do the bank's conclusions concerning countries and portfolios appear to be reasonable in light of information available from other sources?

3. Evaluate the adequacy of the documentation supporting the bank's country risk management decisions. Consider

- Whether the bank's country risk files include (at a minimum) a recent analysis of country risk, the bank-assigned rating of country risk, authorized types of activities, and approved limits on exposure.
- Why the bank has waived the analysis of any countries in which it is exposed (if it has done so).

4. Evaluate the bank's system for assigning country risk ratings. Consider

- The rating category definitions used.
- Whether ratings differentiate among types of exposures (e.g., trade vs. non-trade).
- Independence (i.e., the persons involved in the rating process do not have conflicting interests).
- What triggers rating changes.
- The rating review and approval process.
- The reasonableness of the assigned ratings in light of information available from other sources, including external rating agencies and the Interagency Country Exposure Review Committee.
- The consistency of application across countries.

5. Determine how the bank factors country risk ratings into its assessment of counterparty credit risk.

Personnel

Conclusion: Management (does/does not) have the knowledge and experience necessary to effectively manage the risks associated with the bank's international activities.

Objective: To determine management's ability to engage in international activities in a safe and sound manner.

1. Through discussions with management, ascertain its knowledge of current policies for managing the country risk associated with the bank's international activities.

2. Review the bank's organization chart in conjunction with management résumés to assess the overall structure and experience of personnel responsible for managing the bank's international activities. If no chart is available, discuss structure and experience with department management.

3. Evaluate whether reporting lines encourage open communication and limit the chances of conflicts of interest.

4. Determine whether the span of control for managing the bank's international activities is reasonable.

5. Evaluate the level of staff turnover and its effect on country risk management.

Control Systems

Conclusion: The bank (does/does not) have systems in place to effectively monitor the level of country risk associated with its international activities.

Objective: To determine whether the bank has systems in place to effectively monitor the level of country risk associated with its international activities.

1. Determine how compliance with country risk limits is monitored and reported to senior management and the board of directors.

2. Assess the level of review for country exposures nearing their risk limits. Is there sufficient reporting to senior management, and is oversight heightened?

3. Evaluate the adequacy of the system for monitoring current conditions in countries in which the bank has significant exposures. Consider

   - The volume of exposure and the perceived level of risk in a country or portfolio.
   - The types of resources used including, for example, in-country staff, periodic country visits, internal research, and external research and rating agencies.

4. Evaluate the adequacy of the bank's procedures for dealing with country risk problems. Consider whether the bank has contingency plans addressing the possibility of a serious deterioration of political or economic conditions in countries where the bank has significant exposures.

5. Evaluate the adequacy of the management information system (MIS) for the bank's international activities. All evaluations of MIS should assess timeliness, accuracy, level of detail, clarity of report format, and the amount and suitability of information provided to each layer of management. Consider

   - Country risk exposures relative to regulatory or economic capital.
   - Country exposure trend analysis.

- Commitments, including type, amount, and level of expected usage.
- Exposure to sovereigns relative to legal lending limits (12 USC 84(a) and CFR 32.5(f)).
- Type, mix, and sources of local, in-country funding sources.
- Exceptions to policy and country risk limits.
- Distribution of exposures across country risk rating categories.
- Distribution of exposures by line of business.

6. Test the accuracy of the country exposure reports received by management and the quarterly FFIEC 009 Country Exposure Report to determine whether the information is accurate and complete.

7. Evaluate the flexibility of the MIS for the bank's international activities. Consider

- Whether the reports are generated from a database that allows reporting flexibility. Can country exposure information be reported a number of ways (for example, by sector, by product, or by in-country obligor)? Can reports be generated on short notice to identify emerging trends?
- Whether management can design its own reports so it can access the type of information about country exposure that it wants.
- Whether reports can be developed quickly to respond to a specific need.

8. Determine whether control functions are independent. Consider

- Reporting lines.
- Budget oversight.
- Performance evaluation.
- Compensation plans.
- Access to the board.

9. Evaluate the effectiveness of the audit function in testing the bank's system for managing country risk. Consider

- Scope and coverage of reviews.
- Frequency of reviews.

- Qualifications and independence of audit personnel.
- Comprehensiveness and accuracy of findings.
- Adequacy and timeliness of follow-up.

10. If the bank uses modeling tools in the management of its country risk (such as risk rating, early warning, limit setting/economic capital models), assess the following.

- Purpose, use and conceptual soundness of the models.
- Reasonableness of the assumptions and techniques used in the modeled scenarios.
- How management uses the results of the models.
- Adequacy of model validation in accordance with OCC Bulletin 2000-16, "Risk Modeling — Model Validation," and consult International Banking and Finance as needed.

11. Confer with the examiner analyzing the allowance for loan and lease losses to determine

- Whether required allocated transfer risk reserves have been provided.
- Whether transfer and/or country risk has been considered and appropriately provided for in the allowance for loan and lease losses.

12. Confer with the examiner analyzing capital to determine whether capital is adequate for the level of country risk exposure.

Conclusion Procedures

Objective: To communicate findings and initiate corrective action when policies, practices, procedures, or internal controls are deficient or when violations of law, rulings, or regulations occur.

1. Prepare a summary memorandum to the EIC detailing the results of the evaluation of the bank's country risk management process. Draft conclusions on

   - The quality of the bank's country risk management process.
   - The quantity of country risk.
   - The aggregate level of country risk.
   - The direction of country risk.

   Also address in the summary memorandum

   - Adequacy of board of directors' oversight and effectiveness of bank management.
   - Any concerns about the level and/or trend in the direction of country risk in countries in which the bank has significant exposure.
   - Appropriateness of strategic and business plans for the bank's international activities.
   - Adequacy of adherence to policies and country exposure limits.
   - Adequacy of systems for analyzing country risk and assigning risk-ratings.
   - Adequacy of country risk control functions, including MIS and audit.
   - Compliance with applicable laws, rules, and regulations.
   - Recommended corrective action for deficient policies, procedures, practices, or other concerns.
   - Other matters of significance.

2. For any issues of concern identified when performing the country risk management procedures, determine their impact on the bank's aggregate risk and the direction of its risks. Examiners should refer to guidance provided under the OCC's large and community bank risk assessment programs.

3. Discuss examination findings and conclusions with the EIC. If necessary, compose "Matters Requiring Attention" (MRA) for the country risk management examination. MRAs should cover practices that

- Deviate from sound, fundamental principles and are likely to result in financial deterioration or increased risk if not addressed.
- Result in substantive noncompliance with laws.

MRAs should discuss

- Causes of the problem.
- Consequences of inaction.
- Management's commitment to corrective action.
- Time frame for corrective action and person(s) responsible for meeting that time frame.

4. Discuss findings with bank management, including conclusions about risks. If necessary, obtain commitment for corrective action.

5. Write a memorandum specifically setting out what the OCC should do in the future to effectively supervise country risk management practices in the bank, including time frames, staffing, and workdays required.

6. Update the OCC's electronic information system and any applicable report of examination schedules or tables.

7. Update the examination work papers in accordance with OCC guidance.

Appendix A

Factors Affecting Country Risk

The debt crises experienced by a number of lesser-developed and emerging market countries over the past 25 years have focused attention on a number of factors that are particularly relevant to the analysis of country risk.

Macroeconomic Factors

The first of these factors is the size and structure of the country's external debt in relation to its economy. More specifically,

- The current level of short-term debt and the potential effect that a liquidity crisis or devaluation would have on the ability of otherwise creditworthy borrowers in the country to continue servicing their foreign currency obligations.

- To the extent the external debt is owed by the public sector, the ability of the government to generate sufficient revenues, from taxes and other sources, to service its obligations.

The condition and vulnerability of the country's current account is also an important consideration, including

- Size of international reserves, including forward market positions of the country's monetary authority (especially when the exchange rate is fixed).

- Type of financing, including reliance on foreign capital inflows (portfolio investments), which can be subject to quick reversals or sudden stops.

- Importance of commodity exports as a source of revenue, the existence and reliability of any price stabilization mechanisms, and the country's vulnerability to a downturn in either its export markets or the price of an exported commodity.

- Potential for sharp movements in exchange rates and the effect on the relative price of the country's imports and exports.

The role of foreign sources of capital in meeting the country's financing needs is another important consideration in the analysis of country risk, including

- Access to international financial markets and the potential effects of a loss of market liquidity.

- Relationships with private sector creditors, including the existence of loan commitments and the attitude among bankers toward further lending to borrowers in the country.

- Current standing with multilateral and official creditors, including the ability of the country to qualify for and sustain an International Monetary Fund or other suitable economic adjustment program.

- Trend in direct foreign investments and the country's ability to attract foreign investment in the future.

- Opportunities for privatization of government-owned entities.

Experience has highlighted a number of other important macroeconomic considerations that can affect country risk, including

- Government's management of the economy and whether there are any significant imbalances, such as a large and growing fiscal deficit.

- Condition of specific industries or sectors that dominate economic activity, for example, real estate/construction or export-oriented manufacturing.

- Level and structure of domestic debt for both the public and private sectors.

- Degree to which the economy of the country may be adversely affected by contagion from problems in other countries.

- Size and condition of the country's banking system, including the adequacy of the country's system for bank supervision and any potential burden of contingent liabilities that a weak banking system might place on the government.

- Extent of prolonged rapid banking system growth and the potential for inflated asset values.

- Scope to which state-directed lending or other government intervention may have adversely affected the soundness of the country's banking system, or the structure and competitiveness of the favored industries or companies.

- Magnitude to which macroeconomic conditions and trends may have adversely affected the credit, liquidity, market, and other risks associated with counterparties in the country.

Social, Political, and Legal Climate

The analysis of country risk should also take into consideration the country's social, political, and legal climate, including the

- Stability of the government in running the country's affairs over time, including during elections and transfers of power.

- Degree to which political or regional factionalism or armed conflicts are adversely affecting government of the country.

- Potential for social unrest, due, for example, to political upheaval, economic distress and/or natural calamities.

- Reliability of the country's legal system to fairly protect the interests of foreign creditors and investors and to control/limit corruption.

- Strength and sophistication of the country's financial regulatory system.

- Adherence to international legal and business practice standards, including the Basel Core Principles for Effective Banking Supervision

(October 2006) and the Financial Action Task Force (FATF) recommendations.[10]

- Adherence to international accounting standards and the reliability and transparency of financial information.

- Willingness and ability of the government to recognize economic or budgetary problems and implement appropriate remedial action.

- Trends toward government-imposed price, interest rate, or exchange controls.

- Extent to which the country's laws and government policies protect parties in electronic transactions and promote the development of technology in a safe and sound manner.

Institution-Specific Factors

Finally, an institution's analysis of country risk should take into consideration factors relating to the nature of its actual (or approved) exposures and funding in the country including, for example,

- Its governance framework, span of control, legal entity structure, business strategy, and risk management plans for the country.

- Its mix of exposures and commitments, including the types of investments and borrowers, the distribution of maturities, the types and quality of collateral, the existence of guarantees, whether exposures are held for trading or investment, and any other distinguishing characteristics of the portfolio.

- The type, mix, and sources of in-country funding, including reliance on short-term, high-cost, or borrowed funds, and sources of contingency funds.

---

[10] Links to the FATF's 40 recommendations and nine special recommendations appear under Quick Links on the FATF's home page.

- The economic outlook for any specifically targeted industries within the country.

- Legal, secrecy, consumer protection/suitability, and compliance restrictions.

- The degree to which political or economic developments in a country are likely to affect the institution's chosen lines of business in the country. For instance, changes in local bankruptcy laws may affect certain activities more than others.

- Susceptibility to changes in value based on market movements. As the market value of claims against a foreign counterparty rise, the counterparty may become less financially sound, thus increasing the risk of nonpayment. This is especially true with regard to derivative instruments.

- The scope of political or economic developments and the potential adverse impact on the credit risk of individual counterparties in the country. For example, foreign counterparties with healthy export markets or whose business is tied closely to supplying manufacturing entities in developed countries may have significantly less exposure to the local country's economic disruptions than do other counterparties in the country.

- Its ability to effectively manage exposures in a country through in-country or regional representation, or by some other arrangement that ensures the timely reporting of, and response to, any problems.

Appendix B

Sample Request Letter Items

1. Current organization chart, with a brief description of individual responsibilities and résumés of key personnel.
2. List of key country risk committees with memberships and titles, and copies of mission statements and meeting minutes.
3. Board, committee, and senior management reports for [time period].
4. Audit reports, management responses, and follow-up reports.
5. Policies and procedures.
6. Strategic and business plans.
7. List of products, services, and business initiatives.
8. Due diligence and/or risk assessment for newly developed products/services.
9. Country exposure reports, concentration reports, trend and growth reports (by country, region, sector, and product), exposures of sovereigns to legal lending limits (12 CFR 32.5(f)), including off-balance-sheet items, and
   a. Distribution of exposures across country risk rating categories.
   b. Distribution of exposures by line of business.
10. Country risk analyses and rating reports.
11. Country and cross-border limits and a description of how they are calculated and measured. Describe types of cross-border mitigants (ring fencing, protective language, and insurance) with calculations.
12. Exception reports and escalation processes.
13. Results, documentation, and validation of modeling, stress tests, and scenario analyses.
14. FFIEC 009 Country Exposure Reports for [time period] and related work papers.
15. Other reports that show
    a. Country risk exposures relative to regulatory or economic capital.
    b. Country exposure trend analysis.
    c. Commitments, including type, amount, and level of expected usage.
    d. Type, mix, and sources of local, in-country funding sources.

References

Laws and Regulations
12 USC 84(a), Lending Limits
12 CFR 32.5(f), Lending Limits, Loans to Foreign Governments

OCC Publications
Comptroller's Handbook
"Bank Supervision Process"
"Federal Branches and Agencies"
"Internal and External Audits"
Director's Book

OCC Issuances
OCC Bulletin 2000-16, "Risk Modeling — Model Validation"

Other Sources
Basel Core Principles for Effective Banking Supervision (October 2006)
Financial Action Task Force, "Nine Special Recommendations on Terrorist Financing"
Financial Action Task Force, "The 40 Recommendations"
Guide to the Interagency Country Exposure Review Committee Process (November 1999)
International Convergence of Capital Measurement and Capital Standards: A Revised Framework, Comprehensive Version (June 2006)
"Stress Testing at Major Financial Institutions: Survey Results and Practice," Bank for International Settlements (CGFS Publications, No. 24, January 2005).